HELLO

HELLO

A Short Story of Conscience

VINCENT JOHN LECCE

Vincent John Lecce

Table of Contents

Chapter One - The Opening - 1

Chapter Two - The Understanding - 8

Chapter Three - The Revelation - 11

Chapter Four - The Awakening - 14

Chapter Five - The Challenge - 17

Chapter Six - The Protocol - 21

Chapter Seven - The Journey - 26

Chapter Eight - The Emotion - 30

Chapter Nine - The Rules - 35

Chapter Ten - The Conscience - 42

Chapter Eleven - The Confession - 47

Chapter Twelve - A Life Worth Living - 49

One

The Opening

Hello.

Hello? Who's there?

Hello. Please, do not be afraid. I am here to help you.

Help? Be afraid? I'm not afraid, and I don't need no help. Get out of here, wherever you are.

You have no idea what I am or why I am here, but I am *here, and I'm here* for you.

What in the hell does that mean, *you are here*? Where else would you be? Now stop wasting my time!

I help with time, not wasting any moment of it. I am here for you.

I don't care whether you are here nor there for me. I'd much rather have you over *there*. Stay out of here.

You could say all that, but I know you are not where *you* want to be.

What does *that* mean? Are you trying to say I don't belong where I am? You're not making sense. And you know no better than I do; where *I* want to be. You don't even know a thing about me.

Do not be afraid when I show you I do. I'm here to tell you there is better than where you are, even though where you are is as far as you have come so far, and that I am indeed still right here for you whenever you need me. And you can know about me just as I know you, but I will still know you more than you can imagine.

You're speaking crazy. *Leave me be.* I don't deal with *spirits*.

I cannot leave at this time. I am no spirit, but I am here to help you out for a little while.

Oh, great. Just more thoughts in my head to get me going. What do you want me to do, get me out of the house and into the world? You know I can't do that, and no one can do that for me. Why don't you just find a place to hide? Go away and stay there.

I cannot hide; I come to you when you need it most, and also when you are lost in your own life. Please allow me some time and I can explain what I am and offer, and we can listen to each other to find what is best in us for you.

Are you trying coming onto me or something? I'm not lost. Go away.

I'm saying the best part in you is inside and you know it very well.

We'll see about that. I don't hand things out lightly to people, or *spirits*, like you.

I am not a person, but I would like you to understand *you* for yourself, and at most to help you unfold from yourself naturally.

Unfold from myself naturally? What are you, a mystic self-help poet? I don't want anything you're giving me quite naturally myself. And I also don't want anything to do with such strange talk that you're spitting. LEAVE! strange spirit that you are.

I am no spirit, although it is quite true you cannot see me. If you listen to me though, although I may seem far off and away, you will hear who I am. I am your **conscience**. All I am asking of you is to listen to me.

My conscience, eh? I don't take no advice or suggestion, even if wise, from *any* source except my own. Just get off my right shoulder and get away from me.

Have you found what you are looking for?

You're abrupt. *Found* what I'm *looking for*? What on earth do you mean *what I'm looking for*? I have no clue what you're talking about.

I know you are searching for something in you – an answer, a purpose, *a guide*. I am telling you your fears do not have to hold you back from me. I am your good conscience, remember? I am here to guide you throughout your life. Please, listen to me and I can help be the answer you were looking for.

All right, creep. So you know I'm searching for some meaning. That's life. So what? You also know I'm afraid. That's good for you. But you also know that I want absolutely nothing to do with you. So, really, *why* do you stay? And why are you still here? Just leave me be and alone for good, all right?

You have never been alone, and I am here for your best interest – the interest of other people. You have people by your side whether it be a person you love or a memory of someone in mind. What my purpose is gives you the best that life can offer, and everyone in the world deserves this truth.

You're nuts.

You are genuine, but you lack the confidence, courage, and independence to go forward toward your deepest, most authentic desires all alone. All that is true about these qualities is inside of you, help is here, and I am here to *serve* you. The best you can be real in the world, the best *yourself* to come out into the world.

You must understand you sound out of your mind, right? I mean, you are talking to me and are inside of my head, and so I am talking to myself – in my head – thankfully not out loud! I'm lost for words as for what to do or say – *and THINK!* What would you like me to do, huh? Play out your role for me? Put on your costume of who I'm supposed to be? How is *that* authentic? Am I just a part of a play to you? Let me go and be. I don't want any more of this nonsense at all.

Listen here, *I know you*. I know you struggle through doubts and insecurities, and yet you are good and strive to be a good person. You hold yourself back from showing your brightness and clarity, *showing* the people in your life who you are. Let this be your personal sign that you are on your way to a better life, a life you want to lead, and I am here (*just here*) as your guide towards that good life.

I knew it. This is crazy, and so are you. I don't need you or what you have to serve or offer me. I am good how I am, however I am; so *LEAVE*.

You are good just the way you are, but the way you are and

the way you are acting are two different ways; one way is *here*, and the other is *there*. You are much greater than you can see right now, but you need to know that there are better choices you can make in your life, *for the best in you to come out and be free in real life*.

Don't you know I am trying my best? Don't you know I am doing what I have been taught from a young age, from the beginning of what I've known up until now? And sure, I struggle here and there. I am human. But you have no right to tell me how, or just how much better, I can live my own life. So – *leave me alone!*

You are a strong and independent individual; however, everyone needs help at times. Your memory is not infinite; you cannot remember all you know at once. You need reminders here and there, and I am that *reminder*. You need a map sometimes when you are lost or need a place to go, and so I am your road guide, and inner map. You can trust all that is inside of you, and I am that *you* on the inside. Please hear me out and allow me to show you my way forward for you. You can do everything your way, and I will show you how you can continue to live your life your way in the world. What do you say?

I say that you are crazy.

Am I wrong with anything that I have said?

Well... no... I will give you that. And I will also give you that you do know how to calm me down, even to teach me how to hear you out all the way through to the end. I can give you a shot, although I don't *want* to completely whatsoever; but what do I have to lose except everything that will not work out for me? It's not like things can get worse for me to be honest. I'm willing to hear you out for the first time since we've "*met*."

Allow us not get so down upon ourselves. I am your good conscience, you know.

Okay, well, let's get on with this. Tell me what you need me to know about you... good conscience.

Two

The Understanding

I am your conscience, your best half, your biggest part, your best part – really, I am your whole self.

That is, and sounds, absolutely insane.

It does, doesn't it? Trust or listen to yourself at all times. You doubt yourself, but I am here to bring that trust and voice back into you. I am your own personal conscience, and I am here for you to feel and respond. Just know you are ready whenever you say so, and I am the way for what is really the best for you.

Okay, so you are my better half. Sure. So, what on earth do I do from here on out? Where do I go, and when? And what the hell does conscience have to do with anything anyways? Do I just blindly follow you or something? I don't get it.

Well, you see, you can never completely know me wholly and truly, you can only feel and sense me when I am there. I am your unconscious mind revealed in minor ways. Your inner words are your fuel for your actions, and I am that fuel for you. I am your inspiration, and I am your courage. I am the way that you change for the best, and I am the one to tell you *not* to do that, but *this, please*. I am your better part, it is true, but sometimes I take up little more than a little bit of you. That means I am not your half – only when you work with me. I love cooperation and teamwork and letting that dream of yours become true, in work, practice, and mind, and with everyone around you. And I love *you*. I truly love all that you are. And when you do what is best for you and the interests of others living their best lives, I am the most happy. I want the best for you just like you naturally care for people. And I am all yours. It is just up to you to listen to me.

Okay, fine. You love me. You want the best for me, too. But how can I let you in all the time like I am doing now? How can I fully and completely trust you in all I do?

You have to listen to your gut. You need to comprehend the subtle messages, and the big ones, I send to you on your way. I am not complicated, but am simple, but not always the easy path to choose. I am your better part, and your love of life, and your dreams to come true. You, in order to live the life you have always imagined, must trust me in your experience and your head; your heart, your body, and your soul need you, too. As unusual as this sounds, it is your way forward to better yourself and do the truly best you do and choose. And *you can do it all with trust in what is yet to come.*

Three

The Revelation

All right, conscience, you got me. And I'm starting to get you, too. But how is it that I am in the rut I am in right now no matter what? No matter how hard I try to work and no matter what I try to say and do, it seems as if I'm getting myself nowhere.

You are here, you are real and present, but you are not always listening and serving your better half, and your whole self. You listen to me when it is convenient for you, and that is why you have been stuck. It is true that you will fail along your way to decency and self-understanding without me, but it is also true that you will fail in between your successes too, even when and if you do listen to me. The way is not always as easy as I am to listen to or hear out. The world is a hard place to live in, but it is a world of possibility. Remember that *you* are here, and that *you* are *still alive*. That is a miracle that you not always remember, and that is okay and all is fine; but is it okay to never remember that you were born, that you were destined to do good and great things, that you *are* great and must remember this on an everyday basis? You can listen to your heart and your head, and I am both of them at once. In a flash I am gone; but I am also here when you need me most of all.

You just don't understand me. You might think you do – you are in me, of course – but you truly must not get it. You think you know what is best for me; again and again you say it. But that cannot be true. How can you know my mind *and* my body *and* my spirit, whatever else you rule over, *and* know what is best in all of these places and spaces for me? Maybe… I can say, I do not understand you.

The thing is you can never understand me completely. I know much more than you can ever think or imagine. Only your imagination can feel and understand me in increments, but only within intervals. You will know me when you *see* me – in your experience when you are listening to me. And this voice is for you alone. To understand me completely is impossible unless and *until* you take me on wholly and truly. In every single step that you make, I am together with your whole self. Your way forward is right here for you, as I am for you whenever you need it.

Are you actually here for me whenever I need you?

I am whenever you listen and seek me, and feel what you have to feel. You can pay attention and understand me as I serve your whole self, your best part, in order for you to become yourself, who you really want to give to others and the world.

Hold on here. Are you saying that there is more to me than just my own interests? Is that to say that people must be a part of my genuine path as well?

Yes, of course! A divide between yourself and people is not so great, wide, or far away as it may seem. Listen closely, and see exactly what you are and what your life has to offer for you and everyone in your life. Please, may I allow you to understand me?

Four

The Awakening

Tell me: what is it that unites me with the people in my life? Is it some grand design, or common occurrence, or coincidence, fate, or destiny? I want to know for real. What is it that guides my life? What makes things come to be?

The simple, and short answer, is: *it is your spirit*. It is your universal love. It is your good conscience. Your positivity that is here, but has been hiding for far too long. It has been hiding because you have been choosing other than you know best for you. You are scared, but the funny thing is, *so is everyone else*. Your life, your truest life, is in your hands, eyes, heart, and mind. When you listen to me, you are given the best that life has to offer. When you listen to others, you get the best that *they* want out from you. The very best of you knows that the greatest answers to your questions come from inside. So, you go, thinking that you are making the right decisions when in reality you are swayed to and fro by others' opinions and judgments, and their guides for you are not necessarily as true to you as they are for their best interests.

Well, maybe I haven't been my best self as of lately... or not at all. I don't think I've been such a good person at all either.

You are a good person regardless of your behaviour. You are good and act well based on your knowledge of what is good. You have tried so hard to find what it is that you are looking for. Now, and right here, you are listening to me aloud in your own mind. You still have a way to go if you are to remember what to do at all times, but I am here to help you throughout it all, as a reminder, whenever you need it most. I am here as your one true guide alone.

But other people *do* have and share their interests in me. How is it that I can trust your guide but not theirs?

You will know the times when you come across someone who is truly out there to help you for your better self. However, you must listen, and be open to listen, to me when it matters most. Some people are selfish; not all, but some are selfish, and full of greed and vice. But you must not get tied up in those ways that people force upon or influence in you. You are good, and not everyone is completely. Not everyone is bad and out to get you. There are good people, and I am here to help you distinguish the good from the bad, just as wisdom reveals what is good from bad. Do you want to continue?

Yes, but I have still many unanswered questions.

Then let us move forward.

Five

The Challenge

How can you trust someone, anyone at all, if you *cannot know* their true motives? Everyone is out to get what they want, so how do you get along with them when you will never know them really until it is too late?

That is doubt talking, and suspicion, and a lack of faith in people. You are knowing already what bad people are capable of, but you do not yet know or have seen the true good that is out there in the world.

So there *is* goodness outside of me?

There is goodness both inside and out from you; there is goodness outside *and* inside of you. There are people who would sacrifice themselves for the best in other people and for their lives to matter for goodness in our world. They love people genuinely and do not wish hate upon anyone. They truly care, and are concerned about other people.

So, how do I find these people? This seems highly unlikely, impossible even – at least in my life.

You will come across and befriend them. *You will*. You just have to listen to me on your ways forward from here. I am not a threat or a bother. I am your guide and truest voice in you. You can trust me at all times because I am you, all of you in one. You can never lose sight of me because I am here no matter where you are or what you do. But this does not mean that you cannot serve me in the same way that I serve you, since you will not get ahead or go far if you fail to see me through to make me real until the very end. You must commit, and while you trust me, you become you in the greatest way, because *I am* you, the best *you* that is possible. Your future is bright when you follow me. It is only then that you can lead your way forward to a better life.

Okay, now this is getting scary. Are you saying that you are psychic or something? You can tell what will happen in my future?

Well, in a word, yes, I know what can happen and will happen based on what you do and how you choose any choice, big or small, within your life. This is not to overwhelm you; this is my knowledge and not your own. I know what is best for you at all times and am part of your unconscious awareness.

So, you know all my correct behaviours and deeds, words, and... do you even know all of my mistakes?

I know when a mistake has been made, and you will, too, especially when it happens over and over again; I also know when you have better options to choose from and what good ideas are with you at your fingertips – even sometimes right on the tip of your tongue. Or right in the mirror.

So you know me inside and out completely? You know my future and can tell wherever I'm headed?

I know that you are better when you are with people, and best when you take time away from them – from time to time – to find a true balance, both in your social and in your private life. I know are good and true, brilliant and self-sacrificing, and wholeheartedly determined when things matter most. You will do anything for the ones you care about, and you know what is best when the time comes to be. The thing is, you must trust yourself throughout the whole process.

What are you here for, what do you really want to show me?

I am here to tell you and remind you that your better half loves you and wants you to know that *your time* comes every step of the way – not just when things get hard, difficult, or confusing. I am there when you need to act or say anything at all to anybody, and when people give you the choice to do something or not. You *always* have the choice to choose your best for you and all of the people you love and care about... and even all people. I am always here for you, and you can listen to me whenever you are in doubt, in any rage, or throughout any of your true fears when they come up.

Okay. That's a lot to take in, but I will accept what you say... rather reluctantly. You are kind and gentle towards me and want the best for me at all times. You know what is best for me without me having to know what is best for myself in my future, though you can give me an indication from time to time.... I want to learn more about you because I know there is something in you that is good for me, but I still have to ask you some questions; I still need a firm answer of what I need to do, and of who I need to be in my everyday life.

Six

The Protocol

Questions are essential for your well-being. They help you grow and they unite you with your better, inquiring self. You come closer to me when you question and follow it. All you have to do is ask and receive an answer from me. The more you ask, the more answers you will receive, step by step, every step of the way. All I am asking you is to listen when my advice and answers are given to you. When you do, you will see I am truly and genuinely here for the best of you that you can possibly imagine. All you need to do is trust me. Do you want to hear more?

Well yes, of course. I go through many downfalls and have been through *much* in my life up until now. How is it that you can guide me throughout all of my life's difficulties knowing what is best when so many terrible things have happened to me?

I will tell you, but you must keep your knowledge of me only with those you love and trust, those who truly care about you and for your best, and better, entirely.

Your knowledge is safe with me.

Life is full of dilemmas. It is the norm and the way. You will go through tough times just as you have gone through before.

Great.

But you can go through them again, and you can go through them better than you ever have in the past. The more you go through, the more you will overcome.

So, you're here to encourage me?

To listen and to trust, to act in your best interest all the way through, I am here for you and here to tackle whatever life throws your way. *Trust in me*. Listen and hear me out all the way: you are *better* than your past. You are *better* than what you imagine and whatever you imagine your future to be. All that imagining is based on your past, but the knowledge of hearing me out is *better* than anything else that has ever, or will ever, come your way.

Okay, fine. I trust you and all for now. But you have got to understand that my past is not as easy to overcome as you say to me. There were many hardships and struggles, pains and sadness, places of confusion, doubts, fears, stress, anxiety, you name it; you cannot just tell me that listening to someone like you, my *conscience*, will turn everything around for me in the end.

You are right in part, but not at all completely. You must listen, yes, to me in all I show you, but you also must act, you must speak, you must try to do your best – *that is your better half*. And you also must *choose* in the best interests of people, which always includes yourself. Your choices are your routes that you take on your journey. They are the pathways that lead you forward and ahead, or far, far back and behind.

How do you know what I want and where I want to go?

I know what you want, to be ahead, to move towards your goals, further than you ever have been before; but, sadly, the question of how is a mystery. I cannot say how I know all that you are or will be. But you must act according to what your gut feels, and what your body says to you. You are never alone – *remember this* – but you are an individual who chooses for yourself and not for anyone else.

Isn't that not according to other people? Isn't that a disregard of people in general except for me?

That, by the way, is not selfish, but in your own best interest... *and* in the interests of all people in general. When you say someone can give someone they love a present when they have no present at all to give, how can they give any happiness to others when they cannot be happy themselves? You want to give happiness to others. You want to give people the attention and love they deserve. What kind of person would you be if you were to throw away your best interests and attention and love that you deserve to give to yourself just because you think you are selfish when you act on your interests, love, and attention?

If I understand correctly, I would *not* be the type of person I want to be... knowing I love myself and my own attention towards me rather than the attention of other people. To love myself, it's true, is not selfish, but loving. To not love myself I would not love anybody at all.

You would *not be you* period. Listen to me and hear and see and touch and smell, know and feel, act and choose in the right way for you, in the best ways for the people all around you, for you! Whenever you are put in any situation that comes to you, you will know what is best for all people you are with. Your situations when with people and what you have to face *will come to you*. But you just must be patient enough and listen enough for you to know when it is the right time to act and listen, and know the thing to do.

So I can follow you and actually do my best? You're saying that I can handle what comes to me while being responsible for my people and myself? And all this happens because I listen and act upon it?

I, your conscience, am telling you to listen and live your best life – in the best of the ways that you ever can.

Seven

The Journey

From your tone of voice and everything you've been telling me, it seems like you really want the best for me. But how can I enjoy myself while only listening to you without doing what I want on my own? Don't you respect my choices and wish me the best no matter what I do?

Well, yes, of course – no matter what you do I care for you and give you all I have to offer. *That* is my unconditional love for you always. But when you do not listen to my advice, I do not wish you harm, but the harm does eventually come, outside my control and lead, as you are not being true to yourself.

So I really *can't* not listen to you.

If and when you are ready, and willing, you will serve the best in you because you want to see more of me and what I have to offer. As your conscience, I am your guide to life. As you follow my advice, you will see the best in you to come. Out of every single decision you make, you make and help the moment in the making. All you do is the best you have when you listen to me and follow. It is the way forward, and you will be brimming with your abundant self in all that you choose to do that serves everyone. You have a choice, and you have free will. But to choose me, you have real freedom.

And I can enjoy myself while following orders?

My advice is not an order: it is your true calling. You are a human being better than you can ever imagine, better than you have ever asked for. You are it! You are the one you have been looking for all along. And you are the best at what you can do and best at what you can imagine. I am telling you nothing other than to act as you are, to do the best that is within you. Just try to follow me for the best life can offer you.

I'm sure I can try my best for that. Please tell me more about you.

I am infinite. I am abundant. I do not cease and am always willing to help. But I am nothing without you. You are the driver. You are in the seat and you are steering right now. But you must hold on. You must look and you must listen for the warning signs and must be cautious for sirens. I will give you an abundant amount of what you need, but not always in the way that you expect or want things to be. Your circumstance is the best for you, whether you believe it to be or not. I am for you and for your future and all the people living within it. You are the driver and the all passengers will bring you light when you allow me to navigate. You are the way forward, and you are the path. But I am the GPS, and the voice towards your destination.

Wow. You really do care about me to say all of that. I doubted you before, but now I am beginning to understand you. If you care for me, you would allow me my freedom and my way to be free for the best in me. I agree with what you say, not because you are always right in my eyes, but because what you do for me is truly in my best interests. I can see it for myself – only if I listen and trust you. But I must ask you this: why do you go away when I need you most? Why is it so hard to read your messages to me? Why only go away for me to come back for you?

Well, you know, I am always here – just not in the way that you expect me to be. I am here for you through the people who love you, I am here for you when no other words come to your head to say. I am here when someone stops you from speaking your mind, and I am here when you have just the right thought to utter to that special someone. I am your mind, your heart, your soul, and your body in spirit. I am truly you in everything you do and everything that you love: you just have to let me in and hear me out all the way through. So, do you still want to continue to understand what I am and what I am about?

Let me think, and think out loud for this: I see you care and

I understand more about you, yes, I really do. But, as always, I have a few more questions. I think I know what you're about now (the best in me), but do you really have all the answers that I am seeking? all the callings I stand for in my life? Can my direction be straight from your spirit for the rest of my life? or do I have to see what is best for me after you leave? I think my way forward is to trust and listen to you, but also to see exactly what you have to offer in my personal experience of listening to you. So, can you be patient with me if I am hesitant to start up and wondering if I should keep going?

Just you wait and see for yourself: I will give you my entirety, all the focus upon you that I have.

Eight

The Emotion

But wait. I have emotions. I have feelings, too. Some are temporary and some remain with me for longer periods of time. When is that you? When is that *not* you?

It is always me. All emotions are inside of you, and I am always there. I am you, in a way, remember?

How about when I feel good with the people around me; is it not my conscience telling me I have made a good choice, since those positive emotions are from other people and not from me?

You can share positive and even negative or no emotion at all with people. When you understand emotions come from you, and are *for you*, then you know who and what matters.

For me? You really need to explain this to me.

Remember when I told you that some things serve you while others do not? Positive and neutral emotions are for you, even negative ones are, too, for your better self to come to be.

So you're saying that all emotions serve me?

That's right.

But I have to know whether they come from a true, positive source or a negative source?

You need to know what they are telling you.

Which means... wait. What are negative sources?

Anything that comes from outside of you, just like certain choices you make when with certain people that influence you negatively, that do not serve the best interests of you or people in general.

Like lying?

Yes.

And stealing?

Yes.

But what about the exceptions?

Feelings come from you when you are serving your best self and all that is best in you. When you are not serving your better self, the worse your circumstances get, and the less they are coming from you and me ourselves. The negative sources come from outside of our best interests, *all* of our best interests. (Remember, other people have consciences, too).

No wonder I've dealt with bad situations so many times… negative feelings have crushed me for years!

Well now, do not take all the blame. You never knew about those feelings from the beginning when making your own decisions at those times. You didn't know what it is like to follow something good and true that comes from within you during those times either.

But I've messed up so many times over. All I could have done was listen to you and hear you out. Don't you see I've wasted so much time in my life! I'm a failure.

Do not beat yourself up. You are not solely responsible for everything that comes to you alone. Circumstances happen to people just by the fact that they are living as naturally as things come. To challenge them and make them either better than what they were or worse than what they have been, or simply to not change them at all, is always up to you, and is your own choice.

You do not cause all of your problems, but you do choose how you respond to them, as you know very well by now.

So how I respond to you is what matters.

You got it.

Now, that means I could remember you when in moments of doubt. Can I remember you when dealing with people during the day? before I go to sleep every night? at any time? *always*?

Yes. The point is to accept that people have their own consciences, too, and people are as they are and you cannot change them; you can only change how you *consistently* react, or respond, to them in every given circumstance. This is a matter of finding a way to accept people as they are with your thoughts about their own conscience, which could be different or similar or the same as the one that you have – me – for yourself.

People's consciences... that's a new one for me. As if I didn't have enough trouble already figuring out my own; now I have to figure out someone else's!

The point is not to figure out other people and their conscience, but to think about how they *feel*, to *sense* what they might be seeing, then to *know* what to do with you. With more practice in following me, you will see who is living their best life according to their own rules of conscience rather than with negativity in circumstance or influence. The rules come from inside them and inside you alone.

Nine

The Rules

Hold on there. Rules? That must be some sort of impediment. You cannot have rules if you are to become free, as you say. How can a person have rules if they are to be free?

There is a very deep confusion about what freedom is in today's world. The life you were meant to lead is much different than you would ever expect.

So, you're saying that to be free is to be confined, to follow rules – *of your conscience*?

You are never confined when you are following your conscience, or even when you follow rules. You abide by whatever you choose, and, at all turns, you abide by something. No one is completely free from rules, even if it is a matter of conducting yourself. Monitoring what you do, say, or choose, everyone has rules they follow, and whether they know it or not, they follow something. For the people who follow their conscience, they know whether what they do follows a set of rules from themselves or against themselves. There is no true compromise between the two – it is either you follow it or you do not.

This is starting to sound so much more difficult than ever before.

Well, in all honesty, it is difficult. My rules are simple to follow, but the way forward is full of difficulties – it is definitely not easy. There is no easy way, but I am, in fact, the most simple way forward. There is no *sometimes* yes and *sometimes* no. There is either a yes or a no. A maybe could come along when following me; but when the true times come, it is either yes or no.

Goodness. So I have to either follow you or toss you aside?

There is no tossing aside your conscience. I am always the better part of you, inside you. The love I have for you is unconditional, a state that some people believe does not even exist whatsoever. But I am here to tell you that your mind and heart and body knows best guided by your spirit, guided by your soul and your conscience. My rules are for you to follow as prescriptions and guides because it is so hard to get through life without any. I am here to provide guidance for you to follow so that you are never lost for words or when understanding someone or something, any situation, whatever that may be. My rules are here with you and for you whenever you really need me, and whenever you are ready.

But how can someone be free when they follow a set of rules?

To be true to you, as always, no one can be free without following something. There are limits to freedom just as there as limits to the best of things.

So, like consequences of actions, I follow as if it were from a cause of my own doing?

Yes. You are the cause of your own good because you, along with all other causes, have made a positive life real for you and people together.

And I am free to do whatever I want so long as it comes from a good source, which is you?

To be free means not to do whatever you want at any given time. To be free means to be yourself, your better self, so that you can serve your better nature. I am your source of good effects that has made you who you are and what you will become.

My *better* self, eh? So, I have to be the best at whatever I am doing?

Not exactly.

Please elaborate for me....

Your truest nature loves to be itself, himself, herself, what you most naturally may call yourself. It is your path to determine what you do and what you will *not* do, what you say yes to and what you refuse to ever do, at least for the moment when following your best self in a given situation. Things will always change, but for your better self, I can be your guide through all the changes you go through with rules towards a better life in all circumstances. You cannot be your best self from nothing at all. Without a guide, one is lost on the way. One can have no goals or ways forward. You must follow your guide if you so choose to, and your freedom is in your choice to follow, or be led astray. From your best self, your own true nature, which is truly the best in you, when you follow, you will never be lead astray.

I don't get it. Freedom within limits. Doesn't that sound contrary to what freedom is all about? And what kind of rules must I follow? My best guess is my feelings, and everything you have taught me thus far.

You are correct. This might sound contradictory for real freedom, but rules are really within our own personal, individual, human freedom – and rules make you free. We all need someone to catch us when we are about to fall, when we are going head first into the unknown, and there are limits that are necessary within that journey. Without limits and rules, we would have no direction, no aim, no goals, no future to look forward to. Within limit, we pave our way, our own individual and collective way, a way that is full of true choice and authenticity. Without limit, we would wander and get on to nowhere really in life. Within limit, we free ourselves from the nothing that our lives could end up being.

Wow. That was pretty deep. But that still doesn't convince me that freedom is within our own constraints. Why would I want to do anything otherwise from what I want to do at any given time?

The short answer, my dear friend, to that would be the consequences.

So, the causes and effect?

Yes. Imagine you wanted to go and live your life eating and drinking all day long, whenever you wanted. You think you would be fulfilled by doing nothing but eating and drinking, but it would cause you to gain weight, become bored and stagnant, and cause the eating and drinking to become a monotonous, familiar routine, a negative path for you and people over time. The boredom would set in as soon as you satisfy your desires, and you would want nothing to do with food and drink after a while. The same goes with living life freely without bounds. Shortly you would get bored and move on to the next thing and the next thing without any thought of consequence or effect on the people in your life, even yourself. The lesson here is that you must limit what you do, for good reason, in order to live your life fully and love your life the way you want to do, with purpose, and your conscience, of course.

I see. You have a way to sway there, conscience. But you still have much more to show and prove to me if you think I'm going to follow you that easily.

I guess I have more to show and prove to you then.... I already know you.

How well *do* you know me?

I know you on the inside and I know you when you are placed in a positive or negative state or situation. I know your habits and I know your idiosyncrasies, what makes you tick, and what makes you *you* after all. I know how you love some people while not liking, even *hating*, some people, and how the good people in your life matter a whole lot more to you than you know or remember all the time. I know what you want out of life, and I know what you want to give. All of you is what I know best, and I wish to fulfill the life I have for you and the people you love.

You know my innermost deepest darkest secrets and desires and what I truly want out of life.... Fine. So, show me again what you want from me that would make me be in complete control of my destiny with you by my side and in my heart, mind, and wherever else you said you would be with me if I travel this journey with you.

Again, your better life starts with me, and ends with you. It is not what I want from you, but what you want from this life you live. You are the end and, in a way, you are the beginning too. So, do you want to follow me a bit deeper than you ever have before?

I've come this far. Why stop now?

Ten

The Conscience

You've agreed to continue along this course to understand me. Now, I would like to show you how your conscience actually works.

I'm all ears. Please, let me know who *you* are.

Imagine you were knowledgeable, completely. Not in a short-sighted way. Not in a few areas and not in others. Imagine you were fully intelligible with all that comes to you, and all that moves from you, in each and every one of your ways. Now: think about a time when you have known something for sure, for certain, with every fibre of your being; you knew it then and what you remember now, and what you remember now is still not as important as it was when you first understood what you knew. This knowledge, this fundamental, essential knowledge, is your conscience, the mind, body, and soul of the memory of your conscience, that is with you at all times. When you forget, it remembers; when you lose track, it leans you back on the right track. There is no quarrel within your conscience; it knows you best and foremost, with everything it has to offer you, and it has to offer your whole being.

So, this conscience, this fundamental knowledge, is what I need to know?

The conscience is your remembrance of things past, in the present, and for your future, beyond any time.

So, you know me and where I am headed and what will come out of my decisions, movements, and habits, and you know what I need to correct and what I need to continue?

Yes, yes, exactly. You know what is good for you on the inside, but there are so many things to remember in the world that it is hard to keep track of everything you must remember. Therefore, I remember *for you*, but you do the real work: I remember your mistakes and your successes, your problems and your solutions; you remember the actions responsible to bring yourself the life that is the best you can possibly imagine. You are not entitled to remember and, for that reason, you have me by your side and inside at all times. You are never lost for words or your actions, because I am there. You act, and I remember, and you live your life, and remember, too.

You keep me on track while I am weak in memory? You help me to strengthen my own?

Not everyone remembers everything when the time comes, but your conscience shows you what is right from what is wrong in each moment – for you and your true morality.

So, when I'm out and about, in a totally new situation, you *still* have an answer for what I should be doing and what I should be saying, choosing, and all of the above that I should know?

Always. You are never out on a limb. Your situations are always based on your past, and where you are now is always the route towards your future: *cause and effect*. Every single moment counts in your past and present for your future, and your future is the goal that you strive to continue on to reach your final destinations. You have many destinations to choose from, but I know what is best. You can trust me, for when you trust me, you can see the goodness in your actions, in your consequences, and in what you feel, all based on me – your conscience.

So, you're superhuman, and you're inside of me. Does that make me superhuman?

Following your conscience makes you aware of what you are getting yourself into and where you are headed. Without your conscience, you would fail to remember key points and experiences that have been buried deep inside you from your past, far from your present moment. But you are here, and your conscience is always present. You radiate with me when we cooperate in synchronicity.

So, when I'm not fully aware, my conscience is always there.

Precisely.

Okay. So let me get this straight. You know every move I make and what effects come with it. You know where I should go, what I should say, what I should think, and what I should choose. Do I have *any* free will if I follow you every step of the way?

A good question. You are free as long as you follow me, but you always have a choice, throughout every step you make, with or without me. Every choice that is made in response to your conscience, that you follow all the way through, helps you to navigate through any situation that comes along your way. Your part that you follow is a part of the whole world, and the whole world *cannot* be understood in all its parts added up altogether. It is up to you to know and move forward to progress in life in the way you were intended, and the part you play affects every single living being that is out there in our universe, just as they affect you. You are the sculptor of your sculpture, the life that you lead, and you are the way forward beyond your own dreams. It is up to you to decide whether you want your freedom or want to fight against it, without insight or inner wisdom.

You really have a way with words. But I still have the feeling that you are not the whole part of me, but something else that wants to dominate all I do, say, and choose. Why can't I choose things for myself?

In honesty, I did not want to mention this, but there is a reason why I am with you all along....

Eleven

The Confession

What do you mean? Are you some sort of spirit, or a ghost? Are you some figment of my imagination?

Nothing of the sort. In fact, I am only here temporarily, or as temporarily as you need me to be. It is true I am always here, but the moment you know what to do, I cease to exist as a voice inside. I am your conscience when you need me; but when you don't, I do disappear, at least temporarily.

What are you saying? You are some kind of thing that comes and goes as you please?

No – I am here when you need me and am still with you when you don't. I am always here, but from a distance; close only when you need assistance. I am present within you, but only as a guiding force when you try but do not succeed, when you *try* to act, speak, or choose instead of acting naturally.

Just tell me what you are saying. You are confusing what I understood! Are you not with me at all times?

I am, but am still temporary because I only guide you when you need me. I am gone or otherwise not there when you do not need me. I am guided by necessity.

Okay. So you disappear when I don't need you, and when I already know what to do, you're not there? Or when I know how to act, speak, or choose anything wisely?

Correct. You already know me, so I am gone.

What? Wait! I have more questions! Where did you go? I need to know more! All right, it's gone... but I shouldn't panic. Maybe I will just think I don't understand and then my conscience will come back. Okay, so, wait... how come I know what to do now? I must understand the nature of my conscience! Is it because my guide no longer serves me that I serve myself? *Yes*... it is quite clear now! *I can* see my way forward and *I can* see my life ahead of me. Now, why don't *I start* this out and *start living* the way that *I* truly *need* to... *intend* to... *must*... *lead*?

Twelve

A Life Worth Living

Could I be so blind before? How couldn't I see that all this was just me speaking... me speaking all alone... *to myself*? I mean, I knew I wasn't crazy, or at least not completely, when I started this out for myself. I was asking the right questions, making the same remarks I would have made if I were speaking to someone else, and I was thinking clearly throughout it in a way I never knew before, that I am capable of. This shows me enough of what I need to know. This is the life I am leading for me and all people. No more putting things off. No more waiting for slack to be given. No more wasting away my days thinking I know what I am doing when I really do not. My conscience has my back, and I've got the front seat of my conscience. I *am* my conscience; I *know* what to do. And I *no longer need it* to serve me as a guide. And *why*? – because I *am* my guide. I *am* my way forward, and a way forward *for you*. You know what to do and what to say and what to choose – and for people, including yourself. Your choices are dependent on you and no one else, but *your* conscience. You define yourself and you love yourself, so start to *enjoy* your life worth living. Now, it's a worthy effort to continue – to serve the life you were meant to lead. And now... I hope you can live a little simpler.

Thank you.

Your old friend,
   Your Good Conscience

www.ingramcontent.com/pod-product-compliance
Lightning Source LLC
Chambersburg PA
CBHW072209100526
44589CB00015B/2451